Jimmy Carter

A Little Golden Book® Biography

By Michael Joosten

Illustrated by Jim Starr

 A GOLDEN BOOK • NEW YORK

Text copyright © 2025 by Michael Joosten
Cover art and interior illustrations copyright © 2025 by Jim Starr
All rights reserved. Published in the United States by Golden Books, an imprint of
Random House Children's Books, a division of Penguin Random House LLC, 1745 Broadway,
New York, NY 10019. Golden Books, A Golden Book, A Little Golden Book, the G colophon,
and the distinctive gold spine are registered trademarks of Penguin Random House LLC.
rhcbooks.com
Educators and librarians, for a variety of teaching tools, visit us at RHTeachersLibrarians.com
Library of Congress Control Number: 2024940865
ISBN 978-0-593-89834-5 (trade) — ISBN 978-0-593-89835-2 (ebook)
Printed in the United States of America
10 9 8 7 6 5 4 3 2 1

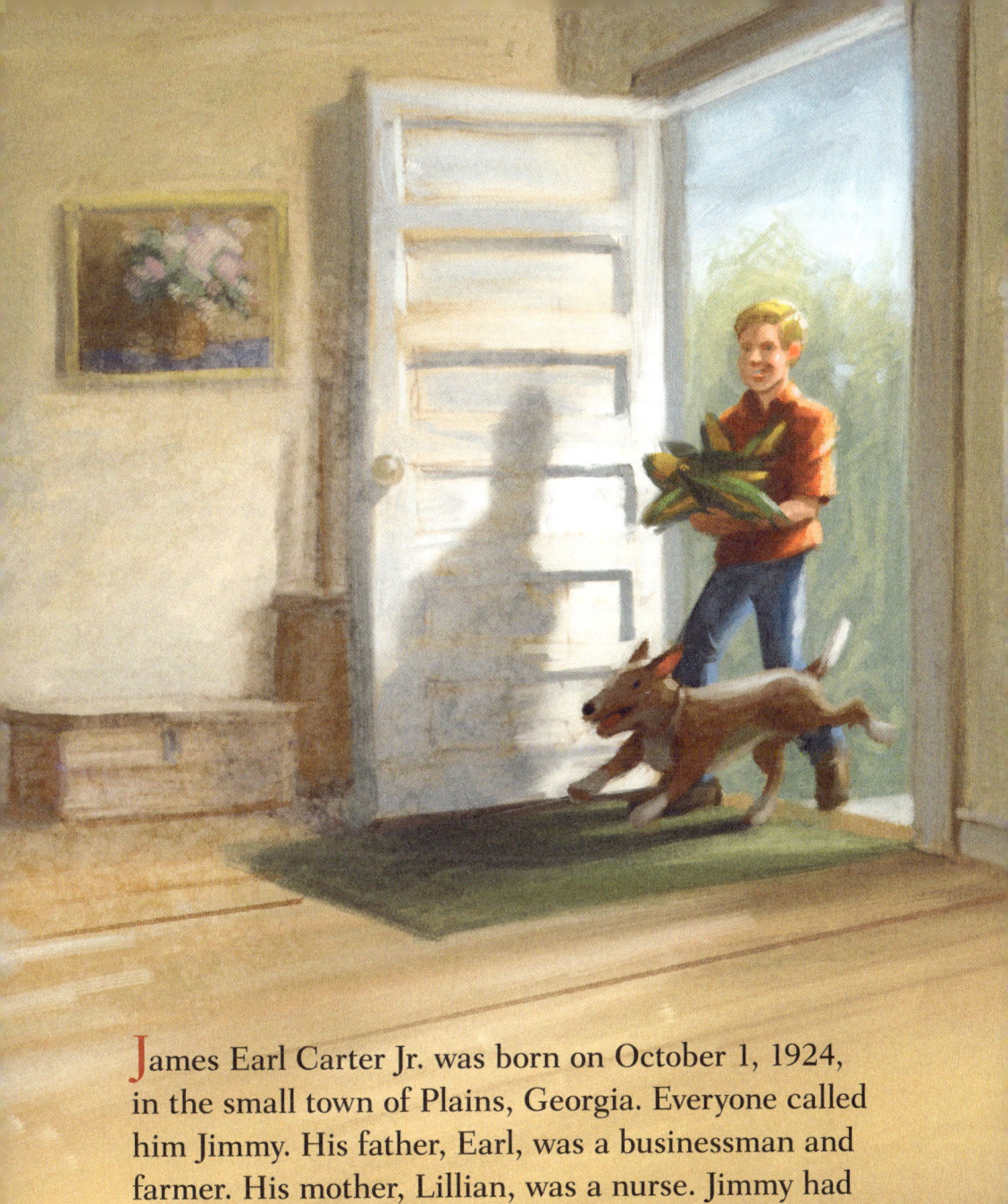

James Earl Carter Jr. was born on October 1, 1924, in the small town of Plains, Georgia. Everyone called him Jimmy. His father, Earl, was a businessman and farmer. His mother, Lillian, was a nurse. Jimmy had two younger sisters, Gloria and Ruth. When he was twelve years old, his brother, Billy, was born.

Jimmy and his family lived on a large farm where
they grew cotton, corn, and peanuts. They also owned
a tiny country store on the property. Folks in town
would come to buy everything from soap to sausage.

There was always work to do on the farm. Each morning, Jimmy helped out by feeding the pigs and collecting the eggs. In the summers, he turned all the watermelons so they would grow into the perfect shape.

Jimmy also found time to have fun. He'd ride horses through the woods, jump into huge piles of straw, and swim and fish in the pond.

He became good friends with Rachel and Jack Clark, a Black couple who worked on the Carter farm. At this time, Georgia was a segregated state. That means that the Black community was kept separate from the white community. But that didn't stop Jimmy from spending lots of time with the Clarks. He helped Mr. Clark on the farm and enjoyed fishing with Mrs. Clark. He often stayed at their house when his parents were away.

As Jimmy got older, his curiosity about life beyond the farm grew. His uncle Tom was in the US Navy and would send postcards from all the exciting places he'd visited around the world. Jimmy wanted to see the world, too.

During his years at Plains High School, Jimmy was an excellent student. He played on the basketball team and was a member of the Future Farmers of America.

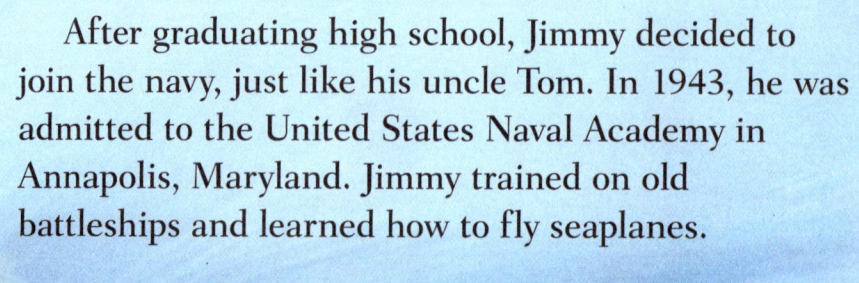

After graduating high school, Jimmy decided to join the navy, just like his uncle Tom. In 1943, he was admitted to the United States Naval Academy in Annapolis, Maryland. Jimmy trained on old battleships and learned how to fly seaplanes.

In 1946, just weeks after graduating from the Naval Academy, Jimmy married the love of his life, Rosalynn Smith. They had first met when Rosalynn was a baby and Jimmy was three years old! Jimmy's mother helped deliver Rosalynn when she was born, and she brought Jimmy to see her a few days later.

Jimmy and Rosalynn had three sons, Jack, Chip, and Jeff. Their daughter, Amy, would be born later in 1967.

While Jimmy worked as a submariner for the US Navy, he and his family moved all over America. They lived in Virginia, Hawaii, California, Connecticut, and New York.

In 1953, Jimmy received some sad news. His father had died. Jimmy decided to resign from the navy and move back to Plains, Georgia, to run the Carter family farm.

    As the years went on, Jimmy became an active leader in his hometown. He volunteered to help resolve issues in the schools, hospitals, and libraries.

    Having grown up with a strong sense of faith, Jimmy was also very involved at his local church. His family attended services at Maranatha Baptist Church. Both he and Rosalynn were deacons there, and Jimmy taught Sunday school classes, too.

In 1962, Jimmy's experience as a lieutenant in the navy, a businessman, and a community leader—combined with a strong desire to help others—led him to run for the Georgia State Senate. He won the election and would go on to serve two terms as senator.

While he was in the State Senate, Jimmy became known as an independent thinker. He fought for important issues like preventing the government from wasting money and ensuring that Black Americans had the right to vote.

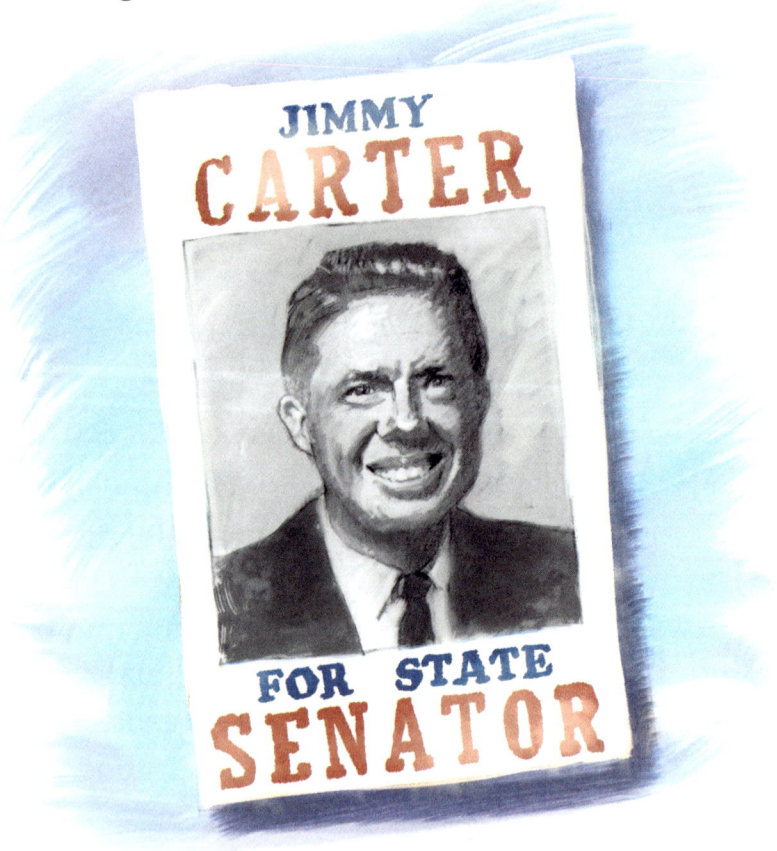

In 1966, Jimmy ran for governor of Georgia. He lost that election, but he didn't give up. In 1971, he ran again. This time, Jimmy won!

As governor, he sought to end racial segregation, protect the environment, and help the state government run more efficiently.

After four years as governor, Jimmy announced he would be running for president of the United States. He traveled around the country for almost two years, explaining why he was someone voters could trust.

His hard work paid off. Jimmy won the election!
On January 20, 1977, the peanut farmer from
Georgia was sworn in as the 39th president of the
United States. Afterward, Jimmy, Rosalynn, and their
daughter, Amy, walked in the Inaugural Parade to
their new home—the White House!

The Atlanta Journal
CARTER WINS

President Carter accomplished many things. He started a new energy program to help the United States use less oil and to invest in solar energy. He even had thirty-two solar panels installed at the White House! He increased the National Park system by adding fifteen new parks. And he created the Department of Education to improve America's schools for all students.

In foreign affairs, he helped negotiate a peace treaty between Israel and Egypt called the Camp David Accords.

Despite his achievements, Jimmy lost the reelection in 1980. He was disappointed, but he continued to work hard and help others even after leaving the White House. He wrote several books, including a children's book that was illustrated by his daughter, Amy. He and Rosalynn founded the Carter Center to improve human rights all around the world.

They also worked with Habitat for Humanity, an organization that builds houses for people in need. Over forty years, Jimmy and Rosalynn helped build and repair more than 4,300 homes!

In 1999, President Bill Clinton awarded Jimmy and Rosalynn the Presidential Medal of Freedom for their dedication to humanitarian work.

Jimmy won the Nobel Peace Prize in 2002 for his efforts to find peaceful solutions to the world's conflicts and to help advance global human rights.

When his presidency ended, Jimmy and Rosalynn returned to their hometown, happily spending the rest of their lives in Plains, Georgia. They enjoyed visits from their children, grandchildren, and great-grandchildren. Jimmy continued to teach Sunday school at Maranatha Baptist Church until 2020. People came from all over to hear him speak.

From his humble beginnings on his family's peanut farm to his time serving his country as president, Jimmy Carter's legacy of fighting for human rights and leading with kindness continues to inspire people of all ages.